Compromising Christianity

Compromising Christianity

Sarah Shelton

Revolutionary Generations Publishing

ISBN: 978-1-329-38879-6

Published by Revolutionary Generations
Columbia, Tennessee 38401

For information, please e-mail at
sdeditio@gmail.com

To my cousins, Sophia and Juliana
That you would grow up with a
bold tongue and passionate heart,
unafraid to stand for what is right

Contents

He has shown you, O man,
what is good;
And what does the Lord
require of you
But to do justly,
To love mercy,
And to walk humbly with your
God?

Micah 6:8

Prologue: Compromised Christianity

As I sat at the table eating my lunch I listened intently to the conversations going on around me. My friends quickly skated from one topic to the next. The random choices of discussion ranged from homosexuals to theistic evolution to drinking. It seemed that each person would throw in their two cents and then quickly change the topic to avoid further discussion.

Normally I would have been content to sit and listen but this particular conversation provoked me to speak. The topic of homosexuality had somehow sparked debate in the group. I found it odd that the previous discussions on alcohol, theistic evolution, and abortion had avoided conflict while the topic of homosexuality had led to controversy.

At first I managed to refrain from engaging in conversation by simply listening to the argument, but after a few minutes of listening I could no longer restrain myself. I am by no means a great philosopher or skilled theologian but what I heard had to be addressed. The statements being made had no biblical rooting and they were actually contradictory to the person's previous statements.

One of my colleagues had informed the group she believed homosexuality was a sin and that the person engaging in this sort of activity was doing so by choice not by design. I agreed with this point but the following sentence stirred up an indignation in me that refused to keep silent. I listened as the person further explained that homosexuals should be able to marry and adopt.

I set my sandwich down at this point fully knowing that I was not going to touch it again. With little knowledge of the beehive I was about to kick, I entered into the conversation. My question was simple and direct but still open enough to evoke more discussion: If homosexuality is a sin why should adoption be an option?

The response to my question was as expected; the manner in which I received it was not. About three of the other people in the group jumped on me at once with views and questions of their own. I did my best to answer the onslaught of questions being thrown at me such as, why adoption by homosexuals is wrong, why shouldn't they be allowed to marry, why can't homosexuals practice homosexuality and be Christians, and what is wrong with the choices that they make?

I was appalled by the views being presented before me. I have been called conservative, by the book, and even strict, but none of those names had ever bothered me until this moment. I felt anger and confusion mix in a way that I have never felt before. One of my colleagues called me a religious freak. I was told that I was too extreme and that my way of thinking was not consistent with the culture's Christianity.

My thinking was not consistent with the culture. Well thank God! I would hope and pray that my thinking is not consistent with the culture because the culture's way of thinking is not consistent with God's way of thinking and if God's way of thinking is not consistent with the culture then the culture's thinking cannot be consistent with my thinking.

I was called a religious freak. The people debating with me called themselves Christians but when it came down to it they sat in the lukewarm side of the pool. The Bible clearly calls homosexuality a sin. Sodom and Gomorrah were destroyed for their sins, homosexuality being among them. When God made one man and one woman He called His creation good. If He had wanted two men or two women He would have created it that way, but He didn't.

As for the adoption of children by homosexuals I will not and cannot bring myself to even entertain the thought. Every child deserves one mother and one father. Every child has a right to one mother and one father. From the Christian's standpoint, homosexuality is a sin, so why should a child be subject to grow up under that covering of sin?

I can remember the conversation ending with the ring of a bell. I stood to my feet and walked to the next class with a feeling of mourning. I was mourning in the sense that what

God had called for and what the world had called for were different things and the world was winning. There was no consideration of scripture, morals, or even a conscious.

I walked away from that conversation not fully comprehending what had just happened. I had encountered for one of the first times a compromised view of Christianity. My eyes had just been opened to an entirely new way of thinking. I was unintentionally introduced to a new form of religion based upon the desires of the heart and the pulling of the soul. In this system of beliefs I found a little bit of society, a little bit of God, a little bit of religion, a little bit of morals, and a whole lot of compromise.

I didn't realize how much sleep that conversation would cost me later that month. The idea of a cultural-Christianity would stay with me until I did something. So in defense of a righteous God and for the sake of wrong and right, I hope to expel the laxity of a cultural based Christianity.

When Culture Creeps In

It was on a cold, winter day that I found myself standing in my cousin's church. I was there to celebrate her fifth birthday. I cautiously watched the excited little girl run around the room with her friends. The children seemed to feed off of the bouncy house and candy. Decorations and costumes filled my field of vision as I loitered by the snack table.

It was in this frenzied haze of a room that I found myself counting the number of electronics present. The concept of a cultural Christianity was still fresh in my mind as I observed the people. I caught myself analyzing the scene before me and pulling apart even the most minute details.

I could see their faces lit up from the bright glow radiating off their phones. Their excited expressions openly displayed the immense happiness that came from these electronics. My wandering eyes came to rest on one man in particular. I felt my heart leap in my chest with a warning. The look on his face was scarily familiar, seeing as it was the same look that had crossed my own face at one point. It was the look of a slave, unaware of his chains but eagerly serving their master.

There was a feeling of devotion and love that radiated off of him. It was as if he had unknowingly pledged himself to this thing and now it was controlling him. Like so many others, he had fallen victim to the vicious cycle of "innocent idolatry". His love for whatever he was looking at was overpowering and demanding of his complete attention. Withdrawing my attention from the man, I turned to see the other guests.

It seemed that there was an electronic device in every direction I turned. Where conversations should have been taking place there was only the checking of phones. There was at least one person at each table on some kind of device. Some of the people were sporadic, only checking their phones every few minutes while others were on their phones the entire time.

The sight of people unable to detach from the world of social media for just a few minutes was not unfamiliar, but it was distracting. I found myself wandering in thought instead of watching my cousin. There was one question that refused to leave my mind: Why do electronics have such a strong grip on our lives?

The answer, however complicated it might seem, is a very simple one. We place the value of electronics in a high position and therefore allow them to dominate a vast amount of time in our day. Now I'm not saying that electronics are evil or that we should just destroy all of them, but I am saying that they are made into too much of a priority in our lives.

Think about how much time you spend each day using electronics. Electronics, although just a small piece of our culture, play a huge role in our everyday lives. It seems that we are neck deep in the sea of social media. We are consumed by the now of today and the up-and-comings of tomorrow. In fact, we are in constant need of updating so we don't miss anything.

Our grasp on information and the events going on around us makes us feel powerful. We feel as if we are in the loop or in control over our hectic lives. This creates a craving that drives us to find out more. It is almost as if our hearts are gripped by anxiety. We strive to be up to date, in the now, on top of technology, and in with the culture.

Aside from information, social media offers us plenty of other distractions and amusements. Games, social networking, and internet entertainment also steal away our precious minutes. These outlets help us unwind and engage with others through social media. We might start off by only spending a couple minutes a day, but those minutes will quickly turn into hours.

We allow electronics to command most of our day because we find ourselves attracted to them. They are relaxing, entertaining, and in some cases addictive. Since we enjoy these things we constantly give our time to them. They appeal to our senses in an intoxicating way that draws in our minds. And hey, if it gives us pleasure then why not do it?

Besides gaining enjoyment from these things, we have been raised to love them. Since early ages such as three or five, we have learned to know, use, and love electronics. They are a crucial link of our society that is handed to us at a young age. We are encouraged to use them and enjoy them for our own benefits. They have become a major part of our daily lives.

While not fully encompassing an entire culture, electronics serve as a good representation. Since electronics are so prevalent in today's society, they must be extremely useful, and they are. So if electronics are so beneficial to us, why would we want to limit our time in using them? Or better yet, why does it matter if the majority of our lives revolve around culture?

We should limit our time with electronics and specifically our culture because it is so influential. Think about it this way. If you are an athlete you spend valuable time training day in and day out. You practice and work hard to rise to your full potential. You strive to be the best that you can be. The thought of victory has invaded your entire life.

When you train you think of nothing but that sport or hobby. You exercise in the morning, watch your diet, exercise at night, study plays, and mentally prepare for the upcoming game. It takes dedication and perseverance, but you become a knowledgeable player. You pour yourself into the competition and in doing so you change yourself.

Your mental and physical perspectives change. You mold yourself into whatever you are pursuing.

You will find that your hard work has paid off when you leave the competition holding that sought after award or trophy in your hand. You met your goal and are looking forward to doing it again. Your knowledge and preparation for the challenge was critical to your victory. You only won because you poured yourself into the sport.

Our culture is similar in this aspect. We cannot help but adopt the mental, physical, and spiritual outlooks of society. We are so engaged and so permeated with the views of the world that we have, like it or not, adopted some of its characteristics. The more time you spend with something, the more and more you will become like it.

Since birth we are surrounded by our culture. We are practically preparing for our future life. Just like an athlete prepares for a game, we prepare for the culture. We study its beliefs and engulf ourselves in its traditions. We spend time in it by using electronics, engaging in everyday activities, and discussing important topics with our friends.

We have been led to love culture; we have been taught to love culture. What do you spend the majority of your day talking about? Is it work, your family, Jesus, the latest product on the shelf, or maybe even that new show? What you love you will spend the most time engaging in and talking about. You will want to share what you like with others.

You wont even realize it, but what you love will almost always be the topic of your conversations. People that know you or that spend just a few minutes talking with you will be able to tell you what you like based on what they hear. So when it comes to your number one priority, think about where your time is spent and what you talk about.

When society and electronics become our first priority, we lose what we are really searching for: God. If our priority is the culture first and foremost, then we will find nothing but empty ambitions and vain passions. Our morals, our system of right and wrong, will be dictated by whatever we give ourselves to. Justice will fall to the law of the land.

Our beliefs and views might not even match the culture in the beginning. We might even strongly oppose what we are surrounded with, but if we are not careful we will start to compromise over time. We will hear the echoes of this world day in and day out, and eventually we will start to believe some of them. Our reason for doubt in our beliefs and the discovery of "logic" in this culture will be products of a lack of a firmly rooted foundation.

We pick and choose who to follow and who to ignore. We engage in what is influential and exciting to us. We follow what gives us a sense of purpose; we follow what gives us a sense of meaning. Every one of us has a driving factor that plays on our emotions and desires. Our pursuit of self-worth is consuming and demands satisfaction.

We were created for something bigger than we could ever hope to be. All too often we look for something to fill the void that can only be described as a bad substitute for the real thing. We were all created to worship, but what to worship is a choice we make.

What gives you satisfaction? There are two primary sources in which one can find satisfaction, one is deceptive and the other is real. Culture offers a deceptive satisfaction that will ultimately leave you emptier than when you first began, but God offers a satisfaction that is filling and complete. Does your satisfaction have an underlying purpose or meaning?

If God holds the key to ultimate satisfaction, then why do we limit our time with Him? Should we not spend the majority of our day in His presence? Think about the possibilities if we gave up just a fraction of our day for God. Slow down, wait before the Lord, allow Him to speak into your life. There is nothing as satisfying as His presence.

When analyzing my life, I would rather it be more like Jesus and less like the culture. To do this I have to make a choice though. I have to choose and set the standard of what takes priority in my life. I have to set aside the cravings of my flesh. The problem today is we practice what I like to call the "ice cream philosophy".

We get our ice cream and then we proceed to pick and choose our toppings. We mix in a little bit of this and a little bit of that or maybe a whole lot of something else. We are so concerned about the toppings that we take for granted the ice cream. We overlook what we really came to get and focus our attention on the multiple, appealing toppings.

So just like the ice cream and toppings, we try to mix God and culture. We want the best of both but are only prepared to sacrifice for one. We try to follow the yearning of the soul while satisfying the desires of the heart. We make a compromise between what we know to be right and what we want to be right.

This is a dangerous place to fall into though. We trick our minds into believing that our motives are just, completely acceptable in God's eyes. We assume that there is logic beneath our values because we only scratch the surface and educate ourselves just enough to know the belief without ever really confirming it as fact.

How strong is your foundation? When speaking of a foundation I am speaking to your facts, to your proof and faith in your belief system. If you believe in something as important as Christianity then you should know a great deal about the subject. Every Christian's goal should be to soak in and learn as much as they possibly can about scripture.

Scripture is the equivalent to God's handbook on life for us. Everything we could ever possibly need or want is found in scripture and in God. There is nothing else as satisfying or as filling as God's word. The center of our life should revolve around Him. Nothing should be allowed to stand between us and our Creator.

The consistent study of scripture combined with the everlasting fellowship of Jesus should stir up in our hearts a desire and craving to learn more. This passion should rest in the heart of every believer seeing as it is the driving force that propels us to fight for our time with Him. Our passion and hunger for scripture should trump every other desire that fights for the allegiance of our heart.

Aside from the basic knowledge of scripture we should know or at least attempt to study some Theology or Doctrine. Use the original Greek translation to discover a deeper understanding of the text or discuss passages of scripture with friends to get different perspectives.

By engaging in the study of Theology, Doctrine, and Scripture we will allow ourselves to find out what we believe and why we believe it. Our faith will grow stronger when backed by evidence and confirmed with the guidance of the

Holy Spirit. When someone asks you why you believe what you believe you will be able to give them a logical answer based in scripture and not just the easy it's what my pastor believes or it's what my parents believe.

When we are constantly engaged in the pursuit of God everything else will pale in comparison. Our perspective and habits will change as a direct result of Jesus' presence in our lives. We will begin to look more and more like Him each day. Our system of beliefs, our morals, our right and wrong, our views of what is taking place around us will be shaped by Jesus.

Ultimately, our character should always point back to God. His presence in our life should be abundantly evident to everyone that we come into contact with. Our standards should contradict society and offend the culture. We were made to walk in the image of an almighty God. We were created to have fellowship with Him.

So what happens when our fellowship is two-faced, meaning we love God and the culture. Culture in itself is not bad. We can enjoy the football game, scan the social media, or read that new article. The question is do you love that football game more than fellowship with God?

Do you spend more time on social media than you do in the Bible? Is the content of that article something you should be reading and looking at?

Ask yourself five questions:

1) Do I love what the culture has to offer more than what God has to offer?
2) What is the number one priority in my life?
3) How much do I really know about scripture and God?
4) What have I compromised to suit my desires instead of God's desires?
5) In what do I find my purpose?

Your answers to these simple questions will highlight what you follow. Is your stance leaning more toward Jesus or more towards the culture? We are humans which means that we carry a sinful nature. We are driven by instinct to follow the culture. Our finite minds will sometimes sell our hearts over to what appears to be passion wrapped in purpose.

We will eagerly give ourselves over to whatever promises purpose. We act on emotions, never really sure but finding ourselves drawn in and engulfed. Our search lands us in places that might start out as innocent but quickly morph into empty idols. We allow our hearts to go out, hoping for peace but finding none.

At the end of our search, when we have given up most of ourselves to the passions of our heart, do we realize what we have done. When our man made purpose leaves us high and dry, we find the missing link. Our worship does not belong to the things of this world. Its misplacement has only exposed our need for a creator even more.

It is here, when we are broken and lost, that God makes Himself known in a powerful way. He strips us of the titles that we have been given by our desires and calls us one of His own. He knows that we will sell ourselves over to the world again, but He will still come to get us. His mercy should not be an excuse to do wrong, but rather a privilege to do right.

So take a look at your life. Find out how much you know about God and scripture. Ask yourself where your priorities are. Decide what you love more. Know what is your final standard and cling to it so that the compromises of your flesh are forcibly put down. Take your time and give it to God.

In Culture's Corner: Idolatry

When I think of culture I think of a group of people with unique customs that are significant to their region. Thousands of people gather together to celebrate a unique way of life that they would consider their heritage. As Americans, we are proud people that enjoy our culture daily. The diversity of the atmosphere surrounding us offers new experiences and a taste of other cultures.

Culture has various proponents that each offer a wide category of options. Categories such as food, music, dance, language, morals, and religion are all important pieces in the huge puzzle of culture. It seems that in all of this we overlook some of the most influential, obvious pieces of culture though. One of these influential pieces of culture is idolatry.

Idolatry could be considered the cousin of culture if we were to relate the two. They easily fit together like peanut butter and jelly, ham and cheese, or milk and cookies. When these two mix they create a dangerous society that is rooted in the modern gods of today and is widely accepted because of the culture's promotion.

Like all forms of idolatry, these idols present themselves in an appealing form and sometimes they even deceive you with their "innocence". Found in every place that the eye would seek to look, these modern gods of today build themselves up from the roots of culture to the branches of our society. Imbedded in every aspect of our modern day lives, they seek the affections of our hearts and the power of our minds.

What is an idol though? Is it a statue of gold or some pillar that men bow down to? How can you even take something so ancient and place it in modern day society? Well, an idol can be described quite simply: An idol is anything that takes the place of God or is given a higher priority than God. Gold statues and giant pillars are physical forms of idols; the idols that are seemingly nonexistent are the ones that are the most dangerous.

The invisible idols that are only seen through our actions, speech, or lifestyle are the idols that command attention and drive our hearts. Knowledge, position, entertainment, materialism, love, perfection, or even yourself will define who you are and what you do. Think about your life and then tell me what the most important thing is. In order to expose these idols for the empty tombs that they are we must first identify them by dragging them into the light.

Knowledge:

Knowledge is perhaps one of the most curious forms of idolatry. It would seem that we all have knowledge in some area of life, but what determines who has the most? It is safe to say that knowledge is learned, sometimes voiced, and most often ignored. The small percentage of this generation is hungry, but they are also skeptical.

When analyzing knowledge we find two underlying problems: insecurity and lack of control. The reason knowledge is so attractive is that it commands attention. If you feel insecure in yourself or abilities, you will feel insecure in almost everything else you do. Knowledge lifts you up and gives you a title that others will respect.

A lack of control will drive your desire to attain knowledge because knowledge yields respect and respect yields control. If others respect you and look to you for important advice, then you will in some way have created control. You will feel important and intelligent. In your own little world, you will be able to direct others instead of them directing you.

Aside from gaining security and control, knowledge attracts attention. Naturally, people will follow what is inspiring, moving, and logical. In this generation coming up, logic is a prerequisite just to start off. To gain their attention you have to either move them with emotion or grip their minds with a strong logical argument.

Knowledge is being certain of something or well educated in a certain area. Imagine how much knowledge would mean to you if you had been searching your entire life for purpose. Just picture this in your mind for a minute. Go through the years from infancy to toddler and now to teen years. At this point you know nothing about God; you have heard His name but nothing more.

Since there is no God, no ultimate filling of purpose in your life, you are empty and hungry for something to live for. You have studied and read about hundreds of religions. Your computer memory is lined with thousands of searches for "ultimate purpose in the universe" or "why life exists" and your whole life mission revolves around your pursuit for meaning.

You crave God but have not come to realize it yet, so you turn to knowledge. It offers a solidity in your life where an otherwise inconsistency is the normal. You are able to feel secure and confident in your position because there is a logic rooting it. You have proof or rather a confirmation that backs your beliefs. There is a reasonable explanation for your core values.

We seek to attain knowledge because we are searching. We search day in and day out for purpose. We crave something wholesome, something that is bigger than us. The reason why there is so much skepticism among our youth is because it has practically been bred it into them. They have been taught to doubt everything because the word trust has for the most part been turned into a shell, clean and promising on the outside but empty on the inside.

At the end of our search for the pool of knowledge, we only find water that is as clear as mud. While the culture has many ideas and theories, there is only one fact that will yield purpose. True knowledge can only come from one source, and that source is Jesus Christ. When we actually open His Word and begin to read life's manual, do we then find knowledge. No matter what, it is always God-inspired, God-breathed, and life changing.

Position:

Position can be described as a place of authority or an area of power. The pursuit of position usually derives from a lack of self-worth or importance. Social status or positioning can have many perks to it. Three of the major ones are authority, respect, and significance. Positing in our world can be directly related to wealth.

Every day we examine others by first impressions. Despite how utterly and totally wrong we can be, we still judge others on the shallow basis of looks and possessions. Some would assume that a man with many possessions is of more importance or is due more respect as opposed to a man with little possessions. While this is wrong, we blatantly see those with more possessions treated better.

A surplus amount of wealth or possessions will undoubtedly gain you respect and authority, but there is little more that this world can offer you past that. Authority is usually characterized by status or position which commands respect and therefore brings the person significance. Position has a way of lifting people up or in other words exalting them.

People respect authority and will come under it if they feel like it will help them or give back to them. They are searching for something to serve that will give them significance. When you are placed in a position of authority you are held accountable for those below you. You are only as strong as the weakest man under you.

Today, for the most part, position is used for personal gain. We strive to be the best, to achieve the most, to be lifted up in the eyes of others. In most cases we are willing to trample others in our pursuit of position. We crave exaltation and the authority to command others because it makes us feel important. When we are in positions of authority we become the final standard.

Others have to look to us for approval and in doing so place us in a position of influence. We find significance in the fact that we determine the choices of others and they willingly let us. We strive to gain control over our world. The position we find ourselves in will determine social status, power, wealth, and control in our lives.

We seek position to fill the gaping hole inside of us. We lack something of value to follow so we create a system of value with us as the governing authority. We cannot find something of purpose to guide us so we find purpose in leading others or setting ourselves up in a higher place. We create purpose by deciding it for others.

At the end of our conquest for position we lay down in eternal rest only to learn that the tower we spent years building, the persona and status we have struggled to attain, came crashing to the ground. We realize that standing next to God we cannot even hope to compare to His majesty. Our pursuit of position has led only to the empty remnant of lifelong work.

He freely gives us the choice to accept or reject Him. He gives us the opportunity to leave isolation and belong to His kingdom. He extends an offer to lay down our ideas of an earthy position and pick up the truth of a Heavenly position. A position that is rooted in Him and His word.

Entertainment:

All too often we give ourselves over to the things of this world, entertainment among them. Entertainment can come in two primary ways: watching or experiencing. We seek the passion and desire to give our devotion to someone or something. Entertainment offers us the perfect chance to experience a rush of life or passion.

Entertainment has a way of pulling us in with a rush of emotions. We feel our heart wrapped up and pulled in with the net of passion that surrounds entertainment. We feel pride, purpose, and power. For one of the first times in our life we feel the urge to give ourselves over to something. Entertainment gives us something to follow. If we are not careful, we will even find our identity in it.

When most people think of entertainment they think of television, sports, or an object that gives enjoyment. An easy example of this would be a favorite movie, new TV series, or football team. We take a simple form of enjoyment and turn it into an idol easily. We replace enjoyment for passion and passion for love.

It might start off as an innocent form of entertainment that is used to relax or excite but it can quickly turn into an idol that commands your heart and steals your passion. We find ourselves captivated by this pleasure and it begins to change who we are. We give our emotions, our passion, our desires, our love, our time to this thing.

One day we look up and realize that our entire life revolves around this idol. We are consumed and overtaken by what we crave. Like a man trapped in a muddy bog we try to fight our way out of the pit of entertainment only to find ourselves sinking deeper in love to the very thing that makes us hollow.

The other form of entertainment is experience. You live in the dream. You work, sweat, and bleed to become that perfect athlete. Day in and day out you train to become a formidable opponent, skilled and prepared for the challenge that has presented itself. You strive to be the best that you can be and then some.

Your simple enjoyment of the game turns into a competition and then morphs into a cruel taskmaster demanding of victory. You feel yourself slipping into the world of love and you plunge headfirst into the sea of sports. You find passion, enjoyment, love, and purpose in this sport. It would be a lie to say that it does not direct your actions.

Your entire life revolves around this game. You work everything else around this one thing so that nothing can get between you and your sport. You are prepared to sacrifice for this game. You are prepared to give up almost everything else for this one thing. You feel an immense loyalty and devotion to the game because it has become a part of you.

Time goes by and you find your purpose in sports. Your identity is found in this thing. You crave it because without it you feel empty. You need it to fill the void inside of you. You need it to give you purpose. So you continue to give yourself over to entertainment fully knowing that you are trying to sow purpose but only reaping emptiness perused by the lack of identity.

Then comes the time when sports and entertainment can no longer fill the void that you carry. You loose the purpose and passion that you thought you had. In reality, all you ever had was a poor substitute for the real thing. You tried to fill the gap with artificial purpose. True purpose is found in Jesus. He is the only way to fill the gap; the only thing that can give you true purpose and identity.

Materialism:

When I hear the word materialism I instantly think of possessions or wealth. I think it is safe to assume that materialism is derived from a need to feel important or the need to be regarded in a certain manner or way. Identity can be directly tied into the need for possessions and physical comfort.

When looking into and sizing up a person's identity there are multiple identifiers that separate one group from another. Ultimately, identity comes down to who you are and is shaped by your beliefs or standards. However, things like clothing, speech, belief systems, possessions, and preferences are immediate indicators of identity.

If you were to meet a complete stranger and you started talking with them, after about five minutes you should know or have a good idea of where they place their identity. You will be able to tell because where people place their identity is often where they place their passion and love. If you truly love something and hunger for something then you will want to share it.

People can find there identity in multiple areas of life, materialism being one of the most prominent. We assume that possessions and image will set us apart or define us as belonging to a specific group or "level" of society. By having the newest car, the biggest house, the designer clothes, or even the most possessions, you can set yourself up to fail.

You will fail because it does not matter how many possessions you own or how great you look if you are still empty and searching for something to make you whole. Materialism might fill the appearance gap in your life or even a small part of your insecurity, but it will never satisfy the consuming yearn for something that offers real identity and value.

You could be the richest man on earth, own the most possessions, or be the most popular model in the world, but it is all worthless if you don't have God. Just because Jesus extended a free gift to you does not make it worthless or cheap. He is willing to give you the greatest gift that you could ever receive. He died to give you life, all you have to do is ask.

Love:

When explaining love we must not confuse or mistake it for something else. The word love has for the most part lost its meaning due to overuse and understatement. We use the word love to describe a favorite ice cream flavor or how we feel for someone close to us. The fact is, to love something you must be willing to die for that thing or person.

Love is sacrificial and it demands you to give of yourself. It means placing someone else's needs above your own even if you know that you may pay a heavy price in the end. Love is understanding, patient, kind, forgiving, and eternal. It is not to be thrown around on frivolous likes or perishable desires.

All too often we confuse love with emotions or feelings. The difference between true love and feelings would be the vow between a husband and wife verses the needs of a boyfriend and girlfriend. Have you ever thought that the glue holding together a girlfriend and boyfriends relationship was self-serving and what the other person could do for you, then you are hard pressed to call it love or even defend it as anything close to love.

In most cases of dating the "couple" is too young, emotionally unstable, immature, and the relationship is usually motivated by selfishness or used to fill an internal wound. Relationships like this usually start out with "love" and end some months later with more pain and rejection. It is a vicious cycle that slowly eats away at the heart.

This form of "love" is based on feelings and only rips away at the person's heart a little more. They search until they think they have found *the one,* give some of themselves away, eventually find out that the one is actually not the one, and then they find themselves hurting and searching for another relationship to fill the pain they feel.

After several relationships that were all originally sparked by "love," the person finds himself brokenhearted, identity-torn, hurting, and looking for something or someone else to ease the hurt. After all of their dating experience they have only been taught how to move on quick, settle for less, only stick with it if it benefits them, and ultimately cheapen the meaning of true love.

In order to fix all of this or even prevent it from happening, we must first look to the original creator of love. Jesus showed us firsthand what love is. He shows us countless of times but perhaps the greatest show of love was when He died a substitutionary death on the cross. Jesus demonstrated that love is sacrificial and merciful. He gave us the perfect example.

So when we reach the appropriate age and are legally old enough to pledge ourselves to another for life, then and only then should we even consider a relationship. Save yourself for the person God has created you for. Hold on to your heart and guard it closely. When you finally do find the person that God has made for you, then love him or her with everything that you have. Love them with the same love that Jesus showed you.

Perfection:

Have you ever spent hours working on a project trying to get every detail just right? Do you constantly strive to do perfect work or attain the highest level of achievement? If so you might be chasing after the idol of perfection, but why do we chase perfection?

We chase after perfection for many reasons. One of these reasons is because we have been taught that perfection makes us valuable or that our achievements define who we are. We genuinely believe that we are only as good as our work and that it will stamp us with an image. In other words, our success is the deciding factor in who we are.

We are afraid to fail because that would mean we are not perfect, we are not close to it, and in failing we have lost most of our value. We learn this by interaction with others. Think about it. When we do something beneficial for another person they give admiration and praise. They like our work and initiative which gives us a sense of value.

Another reason we strive after perfection is for the feeling that it gives us. It has a way of making us feel needed and appreciated. The need to feel wanted can be created when you have been called worthless or unimportant. We seek to prove others wrong by becoming something they could never dream to be. We try to attain perfection and in doing so worth.

No one wants to be labeled as worthless and that is why we see so many people running after perfection. They find their value in it and sometimes misplace their identity as well. They might even think they are worthless or unwanted. They tell themselves that their ability to achieve some form of perfection makes them valuable.

We seek perfection because it makes us unique or needed in a world where flaws are otherwise regular. We dedicate our lives to attaining perfection only to realize that perfection is simply unattainable. So after all of our hard work and sacrifice we find ourselves dropping to our knees in failure. Our system of value has collapsed with only one revelation.

The discovery that humans can never be perfect lands a crushing blow to our image. We have failed. There can only be one perfect man, and He reigns over everything. The good news is that He came and died for an imperfect man. He looked at His creation, all of his flaws and failures, and welcomed him in with open arms.

You:

Self-absorbency is perhaps one of the biggest idols is today's culture. It is the love of self, the desire to fulfill one's own desires, the pursuit of self-service. It is the pride and blindness to place yourself over others. To idolize yourself means you value who and what you are over everything and everyone else. You become like a god in your own mind.

Service to self is usually characterized by hurt or low self-esteem. Either a person has been hurt in relationships and is now only looking out for himself or he has low self-esteem and only pledges loyalty to himself in order to avoid any pain that could result as a product of a relationship. They are afraid to be hurt again.

For a person to dedicate themselves to self-service there had to have been some kind of offense that has taken place. Maybe it was not just one offense but multiple. Whatever the reason, we find the propelling factor to be an attitude rooted in, I've been hurt before so this time I will take care of myself and if anyone gets in my way then I will make sure I get what I need before them.

We all carry scars and some run deeper than others. A scar left behind from a broken relationship or betrayal in a central friendship can leave lasting effects. The wound might have healed but the scar still hurts you. It is a constant reminder of pain that serves as a warning to any act that would cause you to exercise trust.

You are afraid to trust another person because the last time you had trust you were hurt. You are afraid that if you are hurt again you will crumble into a pile of ashes to be trampled on by others. So you don't chance it, you sit all alone and take care of number one. You isolate yourself only allowing yourself the occasional shallow friendship.

Another reason we serve ourselves is because we have been taught to serve ourselves. Outlets such as television, books, internet, family and friends can influence us. If we are not careful we will find ourselves adopting the attitudes and characteristics of what we are consuming on a daily basis. What we like and spend time around will define who and what we become.

If we watch, look at, and are around things or people that have an attitude of self-absorbency then we will eventually adapt to some of their characteristics. We will find ourselves growing more selfish in nature and seeking to serve ourselves above others. This attitude will eventually leave us with little to no friendships, a poor outlook on life, and ultimately an empty feeling.

When and only when we lay down our desires for the betterment of another do we find peace and something that it worth pursuing. We learn self-sacrifice from the original inventor. Jesus Christ demonstrated self-sacrifice when He laid down His life for us. He gave up life so that we could pick ours up. He showed us how to treat others, as if they were more important than our life.

The Idol Conclusion

So what is the underlying root for idolatry? The underlying root is the pursuit and desire for purpose. We were created to serve. It is hardwired into us that we were made to glorify and give ourselves to something bigger than ourselves. Deep inside we know we need someone or something to give ourselves to. We crave service.

That might sound kind of crazy right. You are probably thinking, why would I ever have the desire to serve someone? I don't even like listening to my boss at work. Well, if you have found yourself in one of the categories above then you are searching for purpose. You are searching for something that you can give yourself to in full devotion and know that it will give back to you in return.

You know that you are carrying around a void in the pit of your stomach that demands a filling. You are trying to fill that void with idols. We believe that by giving ourselves to something we will find purpose, passion, and peace. In reality, all we find is a void that steadily grows deeper and wider. We waste our devotion on earthly things.

So we were created for devotion and passion to serve one God. That is our purpose. We spend so much time giving of ourselves that we look over the real reason for our being. We were created to know, love, and serve an almighty God. He gave of Himself (literally) when He died on the cross. Even now He is extending an invitation to us.

He calls out to us to come and serve Him. He is showing us where to put our devotion and in exchange He will give us purpose. It is up to us to run after Him with all that we are. We were created to love Him and to give of everything we have to Jesus. He is the only way to find real purpose.

So where do idols leave us?

Well, idols will ultimately leave us hollow inside. For a time they will give us what seems like passion, but it is just a mirage in the dry desert of our search for purpose. It is a cruel trick that will take you from one emotional roller coaster to the next, promising purpose but only delivering death.

Idols will always leave you emptier than when you first began your search for purpose. They have a way of attaching themselves, draining you of life, then leaving you behind to pick up the pieces until you move on to the next idol. It is a cruel cycle that will demand your heart, control your emotions, then spit you out to relive the entire process.

Is it normal for our love and worship to be placed in someone or something beside God?

The fact that we are human will ultimately lead us to stumble and sometimes give our heart over to things that are not of God. It is in our nature to love the dark and despise the light. Deep down we want to do what makes us feel good. When we come to Christ we find a new perspective. We desire to please God and have fellowship with Him.

Our heart changes and desires to turn from the darkness that we are surrounded by or are living in. In plainer words- when we accept God we bury the old man and step into the new one. We do not desire the old self because we have been shown something greater. We discover real passion and a life full of purpose, not just an empty promise.

Where should our love and passion really be?

Since we were created by an almighty God, we should place our love and purpose in Him. He formed us from the dust of the earth, gave us life and passion but we trespassed against Him. So in order to reconcile with His creation, God sent His only son to die in our place. He did so willingly knowing that our only chance to ever be with Him again was through the shedding of pure, righteous, and holy blood.

So we were extended a second chance; a chance to leave the darkness behind and run to the light. We were created to serve Him so it is only fitting to give all of ourselves to Jesus. We will find that when we do, we ultimately find purpose and in purpose we will find an unearthly passion that denies the very laws of human nature.

How do idols affect our outlook on life?

Idols affect our outlook on life because they become our life. (Or at least a huge portion of our life) We give of ourselves day in and day out, looking for something in return but only finding emptiness. We push ourselves deeper into the trap of idols by indulging our every desire. We strive after them with relentless pursuit.

Our belief that something or someone can give us purpose or passion only creates a hole in our heart that grows bigger each day. Then one day we look up and realize that our pursuit was worthless. It only left us hollow and hurting. By then our outlook on life has changed and with it our character. We became what we spent years chasing, emptiness.

Why do we change for our idols?

We change for idols because we are surrounded by them. What do you do if you really like or enjoy someone or something? You spend time engaging with that person or activity. You surround yourself with that thing and if you idolize it then you wish to be like it.

If you spend so many hours with something then you will gradually become like that thing. Your perspective, attitude, morals, and habits will change to serve whatever you give yourself to. It will rub off on you and before you know it you will become an embodiment of your idol. You wont even realize it at first but one day you will look in the mirror and instead of seeing your face you will only see the idol that you have claimed as your own.

Who do you serve?

Now that we have shed some light on the idols of today, who do you serve? Do you serve idols, God, or is it a compromise between both? It should be cut clear if you serve idols or God but to say you compromise between both (my favorite is when people say they are "balancing" both) is irrational. You cannot serve idols and God at the same time, you must choose either one or the other.

God is clear that He will not share His affection with any other gods. He desires all of you, not just some of you. So if you claim to serve both in a nice little balance then do some reevaluating. Deep down you will love one and hate the other because idols and God are opposing forces fighting for your heart. To love one means that you stand by it and if you stand by it then you will love what it loves and hate what it hates. So who do you serve?

Changing for the Culture

I believe it is safe to say that you are influenced by what you are around. What you absorb on a regular basis will eventually come out in how you think, act, and behave. In order to demonstrate this and gain a better understanding of influence on a person's character I conducted an experiment with my fellow peers. At the time they were unaware of the experiment I was testing on them but after a quick explanation they were all laughing at the idea.

I started the experiment on a Monday. As I walked into school and made my way up the steps to math class, I debated on what to say. The idea I had was to come into class each day for a period of weeks and greet my peers by saying a certain phrase or word. Naturally, I decided upon a single word that had no significance other than being random.

So, as I opened the door and walked into class I found myself staring back at a few of my peers. Most of them just took a quick glance to see who it was before returning to their work but a few voiced their good mornings to me. I responded by saying, “blue.” I received more than a few confused stares. A few laughs and questions were voiced my way but I deflected them and went about my business.

I continued to walk into class every morning and repeat the word blue as a greeting. As a few weeks went by the other students in my class slowly began to accept the greeting as normal. On the twenty-second day of the experiment I walked into class and was greeted by one of my peers with the word blue. I responded with the same and then sat down while quietly having a mental victory.

As I went over my notes on the experiment I laughed to myself. Although the greeting I had chosen was of little significance, it was quickly adopted by the peers in my class. They did not know what it meant, they were unaware of why they were really saying it, and yet they quickly took it as their own and began to do as I did simply because I was doing it.

I found this to be both humoring and scary. It amused me because I was able to sway their actions based upon my repetitive example. In the time frame of only a few weeks I had changed their thinking to match my own based upon nothing more than a statement that was repeated and ingrained into their memory.

This victory was not enough for me though. The experiment was not over yet. I had to know why they followed my example and what their thoughts were on the experiment. I needed to know why they chose to mimic my greeting without any knowledge or understanding as to what it meant. The answers, though not unexpected, were disappointing.

The first student to have repeated my greeting explained that she simply followed my greeting because after a few weeks it had become the normal and since I was doing it it must be acceptable. She further explained that at first it was strange but it transformed into something acceptable after a few weeks and then it became the normal after a few more.

Another student said that he repeated the phrase because he had been hearing it for a number of weeks and then other students began to use it. He found himself voicing the greeting before he knew what he was saying. "It just sorta slipped out," said student 4. He believes that he said the phrase because after hearing it for a few weeks straight it was familiar to him.

The purpose of this experiment was not to offend or embarrass anyone but rather show what a continual consumption of society can do to a person. From the moment we are born, we are told that we are unique or different in some way to everyone else around us. The thing is, while we might be individualistic, we have adopted our views from other people, places, and things.

Adopting beliefs or traditions is not something forced upon us as much as it is chosen by our desires and understanding. We consume what we are around and ultimately what we respect. We know there is something bigger than ourselves that is worth living for and we see things everyday that we wish we could be because we desire something better than this world has to offer but we have no way to obtain it.

We place our image, our lifestyle, our attention in other things that we desire to be like. We strive to be different, to stand out. Average and normalcy are not the lives most people want to lead. We want to feel significant; we want to make an impact. Our desire to become better or to achieve what we define as success will dictate where most of our time goes.

Our view on life and society in particular will determine what we do and what our standards are. Our jobs, friends, hobbies, and interests will all stem from our outlook on life. We strive to become better or significant and in doing so change for our culture. We morph ourselves into a persona or a state of definition based upon our desires and lusts of the heart.

We spend time here and there, hoping to become one thing, but more than often becoming another. We find ourselves drawn in by desires, and left to transform into the image of someone else. We adopt morals, religion, standards, and so much more from the influences around us. If we are not careful our individualism becomes defined by another which actually makes us nothing more than a weak clone of someone else.

In essence, we give up our unique destiny for the dream of becoming someone else. Our desires will dictate our lifestyle which will ultimately dictate us. We will become the image of another, the dreams, hopes, and desires of a stranger all for the sake of want. You acquire pieces of other people or material possessions in order to create one thing: yourself.

If what we do and are around will eventually become who we are or dictate what we believe, then logically the things our time is spent on will dictate what we love and who we serve. We will love one thing and hate anything else that sets itself up against that belief. We will change to accommodate our desires and habits.

When we lose ourselves to things of little meaning, we will forget just how great the Father is. We will fight for perishable ideals and give ourselves over to the masses of intellect, desire, and idolatry. Our perception of God and His Word will become clouded like a thick fog hanging over a lake. We will compromise our belief system to accommodate the desires of our heart.

When we compromise and turn from God toward our own desires a degeneration will set in. We will find that compromise in one area of our life has set off a trip wire effect that springs forth a flood of compromises all starting as small but growing into huge backwards steps. We lose sight of the big picture and settle for the small one. We downplay the effects but deep inside know that we have changed. We have compromised.

When this degeneration sets in it will attack three primary places: heart, mind, and soul. These three simple categories will define our basic everyday decisions. You see, the heart gravitates to its desires, the mind logically justifies your heart's actions, and the soul reaps the harvest which will be displayed in your thoughts and actions.

The result of this compromise is the watering down of the gospel. Not to point any fingers, but the American church can be used as an example here. I do not speak of the churches in America as if they were all acting this way, but I do speak to the churches that have allowed themselves to lose the real meaning of the gospel.

The American church, as a generalization, has given itself over to the very things that God hates and there is not even an inkling of sin in their own view. They see their actions as justified; maybe it is desensitization or just simply condoned sin ingrained by repetition, but whatever the case, it has to stop. The church cannot behave in the manner that it is.

As God's people, we are given the privilege of carrying Him to the world. Since we are labeled as Christians, we are held to a higher standard and are viewed in a more critical light. The world expects more out of us because they know that if Christ is real, He will be clearly seen in us. The problem with this is that Christians are human and capable of sin.

Sin is going to happen because that is what happens when an infinite, perfect God gives the finite, imperfect man the ability to choose. God allows us freedom to make decisions in our life pertaining to right and wrong. Since we are imperfect, we will undoubtedly sin. This can present a problem if you are under the microscope for the whole world to see.

As if sin and man's imperfection were not bad enough, we have the lovely ability to repeat sin. The problem I have is not with the discovery of sin but the condonement of that sin. As a body, we have grown to engage in sin actively and condone it. I have found this discovery to not only be repulsive but to be illogical as well.

I point the finger at no man when I speak on these matters except for the one that takes them to practice. I am not one to blame others without first acknowledging my own part of the play, so I will admit that I have caught myself partaking of these offenses before. I resorted to abandoning all familiarity with these things so that I may not live as the world anymore, but I am still human and I will still sin because I am not perfect.

I have seen the idols of this generation and it scares me. It seems that our youth have taken more of the culture to heart than they have their God. I know men who profess Christ only to turn around and engage in immorality, profanity, and things that are displeasing to the Lord. How can it be that we justify men who profess Christ but deny everything He stands for?

It is as if we go to church two hours on Sunday and one hour on Wednesday with the notion that we have fulfilled our weekly Jesus quota. Going to church does not mean you are saved. Singing songs and reading your Bible once a week does not mean you are saved. Not even the profession of your lips can save you. Faith in Jesus Christ alone is the only way to be saved.

What troubles me is the fact that we have men walking around, claiming to be Christians when it is clear that they are not. I cannot simply condone a man's sin when he is so blatantly forthright with it. The other half of the equation is full of Christians who live in sin and act as though they are justified in their actions. I find it hard to see how a man can claim to love both God and the world.

When put to the test, the condition of his heart is easily identified. A man overflowing with worldly knowledge while starving for spiritual knowledge cannot love God with all his heart if he does not know God. Christians are supposed to be followers of Christ, not followers of Netflix, or football, or Instagram, or meaningless passions. We are not called to give God a fraction of our heart, mind, and soul; we are called to give God all of our heart, mind, and soul.

When we withhold ourselves from God, we give up our right to experience the fullness of what He has for us. In short, we rob ourselves of His goodness. When we compromise our beliefs and change for our culture, we will find the conditions of our hearts shifting to accommodate the new love. We will start to view God's law differently and it will eventually be transformed to fit our own will.

Now, to see some examples of how a man can twist God's law to fit his own, I have asked my friends to compile a list of modern issues withing the church. Out of this list, I have chosen a few good examples of compromise that I believe to be errant. While there is a good amount of examples to be addressed, I will only speak on a few.

Every individual, including me, has an opinion. Some opinions are shallow based while others are deep, some are logical while others are prejudice, some are factual while others are presumed, some are taught while others are learned. Whatever the case, we are all opinionated in some way. Since we are all opinionated and will no doubt already have a strong stance on these next few topics, I will have to ask you to try and be as unbiased as possible.

I will defend both sides of the argument and provide biblical support, if there is any, in my findings. However, my hermeneutics and exegesis may be different from yours. So, I may have a varying opinion that stems from my own beliefs and interpretation of the text. Still, I will try to accurately analyze these current issues within the church.

For this younger generation, we are always seeking to answer the unanswerable. While this drive to succeed where others have failed can be used for great things, it can also become a stumbling block to the intellect. When we simply cannot accept an answer or must have a logical grasp imbedded in scientific research, we can often find ourselves treading dangerous mind waters.

These dangerous waters will be filled with the pirates of philosophy, the sharks of science, or the tremors of theology. Naturally, we are drawn in by that which is deeper than average, knowing that the mystery is calling out to be solved. Among the vast sea of mysteries there is a category that draws in the Christian known as theistic evolution.

Theistic evolution is the theory that God created mankind through the process of evolution. I consider this a compromise as you can see by the name. It is the attempt to jam creation and evolution together in hopes of appeasing both sides. This, however, cannot be done since the two are very different. For God will not share His credit with anyone or anything. He alone is creator, and He created us in a unique way.

When dealing with the theory of theistic evolution, we must carefully analyze every part. Lets start off with the word "purpose". I believe that when God moves He has a purpose in mind. This is demonstrated when He created Adam and Eve to one day bring glory to Himself, when He raised up Moses to bring about the exodus from Egypt, or when He sent His son here in order to take our place. So since God is a God of purpose and order, He cannot be random.

God created man with a purpose in mind: that he would one day give glory back to his Creator and have fellowship with Him. Theistic evolution acknowledges randomness when it states that God used the animals to evolve into humans. There is no order. God would have had to create the animals and let them alone to change into humans.

Another aspect to look at is time. When God speaks, His words immediately have an effect. Theistic evolution has no time frame seeing as evolution is supposedly a long process. We see where God's words take immediate response in Psalm 33:6, "By the word of the Lord the heavens were made, And all the host of them by the breath of His mouth."

Another verse to bring up is Genesis 1:24, "Then God said, "Let the earth bring forth the living creatures according to its kind: cattle and creeping thing and beast of the earth, each according to its kind"; and it was so." This verse is important because it shows that God differentiated between animals and man. He made them according to their own kind, meaning that they will reproduce after their kind. Animals are animals and humans are humans, two very different creations.

We can continue this train of thought with Genesis 1:26-27, "Then God said, Let us make man in Our image, according to Our likeness: let them have dominion over the fish of the sea, over the birds of the air, and over the cattle, over all the earth and over every creeping thing that creeps on the earth." So God created man in His own image; in the image of God He created him; male and female He created them."

This plainly states that God created man after His own image in His likeness, not after the likeness of an animal or after one of His other creations. For God did not say that He created the heavens, the fish, the plants, the animals, He did not say that He created anything in His likeness except for man. Therefore, man is unique and gifted with the image of His Creator whereas animals are not.

Theistic evolution could also be challenged in that there is an insufficient fossil record. In other words there is no proof that any animal evolved, maybe animals adapted, but they did not evolve. If this theory is true, then why are animals not still evolving and why have we never seen one evolve? Another problem is that animal organs are too complex for us to understand. We still do not have a clear grasp on them so how can we even be sure they were able to evolve?

As for the defense of theistic evolution, all I could find were two points with the first being Genesis 1:20, "Then God said, "let the waters abound with an abundance of living creatures, and let birds fly above the earth across the face of firmament of the heavens." Some would argue that this displays how god could have used the waters to bring forth life through evolution.

There is one small problem with this argument though: the life in the water was not human. The life in the water was that of sea creatures as we see in Genesis 1:21, "So God created great sea creatures and every living thing that moves, with which the waters abounded, according to their kind, and every winged bird according to its kind. And God saw that it was good."

This means that God filled the water with sea life and as we see again. He did so according to its kind. So yes, God filled the waters with life but it was not an evolutionary process that He described in Genesis. God was still creating the home for man to live in and that included the creation of the seas and the animals in them.

The second point defending theistic evolution is the fact that God commands the earth to bring forth and it does. Some would reason that the Lord told the earth to bring about life and it did so through the process of evolution but that is not so. God did command but that command was immediately answered by His own display of glory.

God spoke and our world was formed. Going off of Genesis 1:1-2 for example shows that God created the heavens and the earth and He did it in His own power. He created the earth in six literal days by calling it into being. In the same way that He called the light into existence, He called the earth into existence.

Another heated topic among the church is homosexuality. I have had the privilege of sitting in on and discussing this topic with my peers. America has accepted homosexual marriage and some church denominations have as well. I cannot support this view in any way seeing as I believe that women were created for men as men were created for women. I believe that God created us male and female and here is why.

Genesis 1:27 says, "So God created man in His own image; in the image of God He created him; male and female He created them." This verse is stating that God created man and woman, not man and man or woman and woman. Now, you can say that this verse is simply stating that God created both male and female but it does not directly say that they were created to be male and female. In other words, some argue that God is only defining genders here.

I suppose God could just be describing gender but if you a little closer you will find Genesis 2:18, "And the Lord God said, 'It is not good that man should be alone; I will make him a helper comparable to him.'" Then look at Genesis 2:22, "Then the rib which the Lord God had taken from man He made into a woman, and He brought her to the man." So, after looking at these verses we can see that God created a woman for the man.

God's intention was for man and woman to be together. He made the woman the man's helper and said they were compatible together. Also, Genesis 2:24 says this, "Therefore a man shall leave His father and mother and be joined to his wife, and they shall become one flesh." Notice that this verse states that a man shall cling to his wife, not a man shall cling to his husband or a woman shall cling to her wife. If God condoned homosexuality, then wouldn't He have added it in this verse?

We can also go to Romans 1:27, "Likewise also the men, leaving the natural use of the woman, burned in their lust for one another, men with men committing what is shameful, and receiving in themselves the penalty of their error which is due." Paul is speaking to the Romans about unrighteousness in this passage of scripture. It is clear that men should not be with men and women should not be with women.

These are just a few passages of scripture that clearly warn against homosexual relations. Some would argue that Paul was speaking about prostitutes instead of homosexuality in these passages because the Greek word for homosexual offenders is *arsenokoite* which is a reference for prostitutes. However, scripture is pretty clear that a man who lays with another man as he does a woman is in sin and it should not go unaddressed.

I have known people who agree that homosexuality is wrong but that they should be able to adopt. I have a problem with this statement, and while the Bible never actually states this as a problem it does imply against it. We see this in verses like Mark 9:42, "But whoever causes one of these little ones who believe in Me to stumble, it would be better for him if a millstone were hung around his neck, and he were thrown into the sea."

This verse is basically saying that we should not cause a child to fall in their faith and we should not condone any offenders. Another verse we can go to is Proverbs 22:6, "Train up a child in the way he should go, and when he is old he will not depart from it." We commonly associate this verse with raising a child up in the Lord, but what would happen if we turned it around? This is saying that a child is impressionable and will most likely become what he is raised in. If a child is taught to associate something as good or evil from the time of infancy to the age of adulthood, then it will stick with him for the rest of his life.

So, how can we condone a child to be raised under a covering of sin? Each child deserves the right to have a mother and a father not two moms or two dads. So, do I condone homosexuals being able to adopt? No, I do not. I do not agree with the adoption of a child by homosexual parents in the same way that I would not agree with a child being adopted by already divorced parents, or parents that drink until they pass out and neglect their child.

My third and last example from my list is abortion. Abortion, no matter how you view it, is murder. Did you know that a child has a heartbeat while it is still in the embryonic stage of development? That child will have a heartbeat before you even know it exists. God has intricately knit together every life out there and He has a future in mind for every person.

Psalm 139:13 says, "For you formed my inward parts; you covered me in my mother's womb." Covered in this verse is the same as wove. So God formed us and wove us together while we were still in our mother's womb. Another verse to look at is Psalm 127:3, "Behold, children are a heritage from the Lord, the fruit of the womb is a reward."

So, God has intricately knit us together and made us with intent. Not only did He create us, He loved us from the very beginning. God called children a reward, the heritage of His creation. If the Creator of all the universe has gifted us with children, then why would we seek to destroy the very life that God intricately knit and bestowed upon us?

At the heart of this argument, the question is not whether murder is right or wrong. The question is whether a fetus is living or if it just a clump of cells making it nothing more than a potential being? Let's look at this logically. It is safe to say that a fetus is growing and changing every day. A fetus is getting nutrients from the mother to survive, but it is still a baby.

Now, if a child is living and growing and constantly changing then it must contain cells. What are the main characteristics of cells? Cells, for one, are the basic unit of life. They are involved with digestion, respiration, transport, reproduction, and much more. Cells are a basic unit of life that live and function. A child is composed of cells even in the embryonic stage of life. So, if a fetus or even an embryo for that matter is made of living cells, then is it not a living being?

It is living, functioning, and growing, so how can it not be alive? Even in the embryonic stage the child has a heartbeat. It is not simply a cluster of cells that will one day become a being. It is an intricately woven child that is composed of many things including cells and it is a living being. For these reasons, I believe that children are a gift from God and should never be aborted.

Many people support the view that it is the mother who should determine the child's life because it is her body and her choice. To that I would say that she made her choice during the child's conception. Yes, sometimes there are cases where conception was not a choice but that does not give you the merit to write off a child's life.

Life is precious. Children are precious. To murder an innocent life out of convenience or hardship is simply inconceivable. In the very least, should a mother find no other options, give the child up for adoption. I plead with you to give the chance of life over certain death. I understand that adoption or foster homes are not ideal, but is it not better than death?

These are just a few examples, but think about how the state of the church would be if it accepted the people's exegesis of scripture. We would not look like the church; we would look like the world. Our perspective of Christ would change and Christianity would begin to blend in with every other religion. The church we know now would not be the same, it would not be Christ-centered.

The hardest part about studying the effects of culture on the modern church is realizing where it is heading. For the most part, American churches have lost the real meaning of Christianity. We have grown comfortable in our apathy and have allowed the advance of worldly doctrine to consume us. We do not view the crucifixion as it ought to be viewed.

This generation has not heard the story of the crucifixion in such a way that it fills them with the fear of God or brings them to their knees in anguish over their sin. They have never had Jesus described in such detail that they cannot help but weep over His sacrifice. They are not told that Jesus had to endure the wrath of God, experience hell on that cross for us.

We have become calloused, and we have become watered down. The compromises we have made are slowly shaping how we define Christianity. We cannot continue to compromise our beliefs to "attract" the world or "fit in" with it. We are not made to fit in with the world because we have been redeemed from it. We were forgiven to be a light in the dark, not a passive bystander.

You Will Know Them

"You will know them by their fruits. Do men gather grapes from thornbushes or figs from thistles? Even so, every good tree bears good fruit, but a bad tree bears bad fruit. A good tree cannot bear bad fruit, nor can a bad tree bear good fruit." Matthew 7:16-18

You will know them by their fruits. You will know who a man is and what he stands for by the works of his hands and the sweat of his brow. The evidence for belief is found in the fact of action. A man who claims one belief must establish it in his actions or his belief is faulty and does not resonate with his words. He cannot speak of one thing and act contradictory to it if he truly believes what he says he believes.

Something that I have seen in myself and in other Christians is this: we are eager to wear titles that we do not bear. We claim to be Christians and love the Lord but we do not actually live it out. We claim God but wear the world. We speak of love but sow hate. We stand for righteousness but fall to wickedness, and when the time comes for others to judge the name of Christ, they will look at us and see no difference.

It is not hard to tell what a man loves the most because he will center his entire life around that thing. He will make time for it, moving around obstacles, rearranging his schedule, he will adjust to fit the needs of that center thing in his life. He will love the thing that his life is centered around and he will hate anything else that threatens it.

It is obvious when you meet a major sports fan, an enthusiastic employee, or a unique teenager, you can tell what they are displaying and what they love. You can tell because it is hard to overlook their clothing, speech mannerisms, actions, and desires. There is no doubt as to who they follow or admire because they have centered their lives off of that one thing.

So what about Christians? What about men and women who claim Christ but then live contradictory to their claims of faith? I challenge you to think about this question: If you were to meet a complete stranger, could they identify you as a Christian within the parameters of a five minute conversation?

Do the claims of your mouth come into alignment with the actions of your hands? Are you just wearing a title or are you bearing it? The book of Matthew states that you will know Christians by their fruits. Do men know you as a Christian or as a man who claims religion only to turn and partake of the very things that God despises?

From the moment you become a Christian, the moment you give up life as you know it and surrender completely to the Father, there should be a definite change in your life. You should begin to hate the things of the world, the lusts of your flesh, and passionately pursue the heart of God out of love and a desire to see the gospel advance.

When we fail to change, if we fail to be the light, only darkness will remain. There will be no hope, no forgiveness, no redemption, nothing left to live for if we allow ourselves to become calloused men covered in the cracked paint of religion who desire to sit on the shelf in the dust of indifference surrounded by other Christians who see through the same pale light that we do.

What good is it to claim to fervently love Christ and live in abandonment to self when it is all just an intricate lie that we have spun in our heads because we attend church three hours a week and occasionally acknowledge the name of Jesus? There is no honor in a man that would claim to love God while his own unchanged, sinful life is turning others away because all they see is a reflection of themselves instead of Christ on his face.

It would be better for men to acknowledge that they are religious, ritualistic, worldly believers that attend church only to feel good knowing that they live in sin instead of claiming and proclaiming the name of Christ only to cause other men to stumble because they claim to be Christians but are blatant followers of their flesh and recognize the world as their real master.

For we will all stand before Almighty God one day, whether we are trembling with fear or reverence and love, we will have to explain our actions to Him. I pity the man that is accused of living his life as of the world and as a result caused others to turn away from Christ because their only association with that name was the worldly, flesh-driven man who told them he was a Christian. I feel pity for the man who looks into the face of God on judgment day and says, "Father here I am," only to hear, "depart from Me, I never knew you."

Where has conviction gone? We lack a healthy fear of the Lord. We see grace and mercy as excuses to do wrong because we love the flesh and are easily taken by it. When will we see that the consequences for a life lived in the category of a "title bearing Christianity" will not only hurt our own growth and relationship with God but it will also hurt others.

We will begin to act as spiritual infants, only wanting what appeals to our flesh, only desiring what condones our sinful behavior. We will find ourselves loathing correction and abhorring admonition. We will only want men to speak to us in a manner that justifies our current lifestyle because we will have intentions of the flesh within us.

It will happen that we will find ourselves sitting in chairs at church, listening to other spiritually dead men speak, gaining nothing more than an empty ritualistic feeling that appeases our conviction for a few more days until we find ourselves repeating the process once again. We will lack boldness in confronting the hearts of men. We will lack the courage to proclaim scripture as it ought because we will be too afraid of the masses of Christianized unbelievers that sit in the front rows of our churches.

I would rather have a man anointed by God stand before me with boldness and offend my flesh, admonishing my spirit, correcting me into righteousness than to have a man sit back in indifference and self-preservation out of fear only to watch me stray from the narrow and set my feet upon the wide path because the only guidance given is the logic of my heart.

In American culture we assume that the quick confession of our lips after hearing a three minute explanation of the gospel will save us even if we turn around and live as a wretch never again to consider Christ in our life because we were told that that one minute prayer is enough to ensure salvation. We have been deceived and we openly accept it.

I am sick and tired of hearing men, hearing pastors even, ensure God's people of their salvation because they prayed a minute long prayer even though they lived the rest of their lives in complete rebellion to God and walked in the wickedness of their fathers. Many men can claim many things, but only few will take up those claims and run with them until they collapse from exhaustion because they withheld nothing and gave every ounce of strength left in them until they were overcome by their physical bodies.

When the church becomes filled with men who know nothing of the gospel or only understand faith at the level of a child, we will cease to function as a church. We cannot take lightly the gospel or the discipleship involved. Salvation is not won by works but it is made evident through them. God is a jealous God that has no intention of only having a piece of your heart. He wants all of it.

When we start to shift our views, compromise the gospel, and water down our faith, we become the very thing that pushes others away. We become whitewashed tombs, mirages of Christians and illusions of culture that promote a fickle Christianity that can be easily manipulated to fit each person's desires. We lose the fear of God and adopt an attitude of self-interpretation suited to fit our own intentions of what should be written as opposed to what is actually written.

Sometimes we confuse evangelism with an excuse to indulge in the flesh. We deceive ourselves into believing that we need to be like the world to attract the world or maybe we have to have knowledge about the world to relate to it. We find ways to manipulate our terminology in order to serve our own selfish motives and desires.

We try too hard to fit in with or understand the world. Think about how Jesus witnessed. He did not compromise His beliefs to attract people, He never participated in sin to understand, He never engaged in activities that were displeasing to God. He walked before God in righteousness and truth. That is what attracted people to Him. He was the difference, He was separate, He set Himself apart from sin so that He could actively pursue the Father's work.

So why is the Church not actively pursuing this kind of evangelism? Jesus attracted people to Himself because He was unafraid to live in complete abandonment to His Father. He was not ordinary nor did He act like other men. He upheld righteousness and extended love to every person He met. He was genuine, real, not some man with diluted faith or partial belief. He lived what He spoke.

If Christ is our example, why do we feel the need to become like the world instead of being separate from it? I wonder if we truly believe that we have to be like or partake of the world in order to evangelize? Maybe we are just searching for an excuse to live in the world and still claim belonging to God. Maybe we just don't have bold men and women in our churches that will take a stand and proclaim what is hard to hear but edifying to the body.

We spend so much time analyzing the world and studying how to become revered in it that we miss what we are supposed to be like. We were never meant to fit in with the world or find belonging in our culture. We were created to stand apart from the regular; to be labeled as different. We are created to be set apart for the purposes of God even if we are scorned for it.

The only thing we gain when we pursue the world is a broken purpose and a smoke screen religion. If we position ourselves to fit in with the world we will fall to the world and it will become our ultimate authority. We will find ourselves falling in love with the desires of men and we will begin to turn our face from the Lord.

We cannot fit in with the world as believers because it has set itself up against our God. The world promotes a lifestyle that cannot be blended with Christ. Can we live in the world? Yes. We are here for a purpose, witness and testify to the goodness of the Lord. However, we are not meant to become the world nor engage in its pleasures.

God will honor the man that sets himself apart and fully devotes himself unto the Lord. He is looking for men that will stand up in boldness and proclaim His words, His gospel, caring not for the costs of the message or the wrath of men. God delights Himself in men who abhor their flesh but love their God. Where have men like this gone?

Are these men sitting in churches waiting for their time? Are they yet to be raised up, or have they been called but not yet released? I call them out. I call the church out. Should we be so deceived that we believe we have to become the world to witness to it. Rise up church. Live justly, love mercy, walk humbly before your God. Lay down your life completely before the Lord so that you might experience all that He has for you.

God will move mountains with your hand, He will part rivers with the words of your mouth, He will advance His gospel through the motion of your feet, He will work in and through you if you abandon all for the call of the King. It is when we cast off the ways of the world, the familiarity with culture, and walk the narrow path that we will find ourselves able and prepared to evangelize.

Make no mistake, the name of Christ is costly. In America, there is freedom of religion, persecution is not as prominent as in other countries but there will still be evidence of it. A message this powerful will rattle the very core of men until it stirs up either undying devotion or extreme hatred within them. Therefore, wicked men will rise up against you and dedicate their lives to seeing your demise.

Should you choose to pursue the heart of the Lord you will undoubtedly be given the decision to endure trials or retreat from them. The enemy will pursue you with vigor and great force, but you will overcome him with the Lord your God. He will stand with you and lead you through the trials and tribulations that you will face. He will be your banner; He will be your covering.

We were created in the image of our God, made to serve Him and glorify Him with all that we are. We were meant to be His ambassadors and when necessary, His warriors. Yes, we are supposed to be gentle, patient, and long-suffering, but we are also called to stand for what is right, fight for righteousness, and wage war on the enemy when he rears his ugly head. We were made to be courageous, maintaining only a holy fear of the Lord Himself.

When we fail to act as Christians, when we compromise with the culture, we become nothing more than another group of religious hypocrites in the eyes of the world. We lose our witness and our standing. We become nothing more than empty men promoting an empty message, no better off than the men we call unbelievers.

Think about your normal everyday schedule. Out of that twenty-four hour period, how much of your day is spent in fellowship with God or His word? Now, think about the time that you don't spend with God. How much of that time would be considered pleasing in God's eyes? Are you living a life that is glorifying God?

Within that twenty-four hour time period don't be surprised if you find some junk in your life that is only clogging up your heart with filth. Analyze that movie you watched, those funny pictures you saw, that joke you told or laughed at, the words that come out of your mouth, and your actions. Are the things that you enjoy, that you look at, that you read, that you laugh at, are they pleasing to God or are they just defaming His image?

Out of that day that you just analyzed, what is the ratio of time you spent with God to the amount of time that you spent doing other free time activities? I'm willing to bet that there is a huge gap in the ratio of your time spent on God and other activities. The ratio will almost never be even. Your time will be dictated by either God or your other free time activities because you will really only love and serve one of those two options.

Our God is an awesome God. He is magnificent. It is often hard to think about how such a God could become the very image of filth and sin that we cast upon Him. It is hard to image how such power was withheld on the cross so much so that the son of God breathed His last. Picturing our Jesus as a marred, beaten, broken, battered piece of flesh is not the image that we revel in, but it should be.

The moment He gave up life for us was when the wrath of God subsided. Forgiven, called by name, left to receive or reject the substitution of our death sentence. Dwelling on this Jesus should bring us to our knees in remorse, trembling at the sight of our sin, realizing that we should be the ones hanging on that cross. We know that death was just a preliminary action to eternal life though. We know that a victorious king would arise three days later in unsurpassed glory.

The revelation of this Jesus, of this story and events, should provoke us to move for the very heart of God. Should our hearts not be stirred up within us and set to flame for the desires of the Lord? This realization of the gospel should transform our lives in a way that we ourselves don't even recognize the life we had before Jesus.

For He has called us His own. We were redeemed with a most pure blood that freely poured out for our sin, our trespasses, to offer up salvation to wicked men. If this is life, what are we doing wasting ourselves on the fading loves of this world? Why are our hearts divided between this and that? Why are we craving the perishable instead of chasing the eternal?

It is as if we have tasted the best drink imaginable and have thrown it out for expired, sour milk. We would deem a man a fool if he was given a million dollars but then went home and put it through a paper shredder. We would consider a man to be mentally ill if he owned a mansion but never used it because he preferred to sleep out on the streets, yet we consider the disposal of Christianity, or at least the misplacement of it, to be rational and acceptable.

We treat Christianity like a lucky charm or a backup plan. Isn't it curious how our time with God increases when our lives become hectic. Or maybe we just keep Christianity in the corner of the closet in our hearts, only concerned with the salvation aspect of the deal and nothing else. You see, sometimes we treat Jesus like an antique, an item of value wrapped up and stuffed in the back of the attic only to be brought out at rare occasions.

We wonder why our lives are not as full when we only give God pieces of the puzzle instead of the whole thing. The problem is we dictate what God can touch "as if we can really do that" instead of surrendering completely to Him and yielding all of what we have over to His hand. We have this view that we are in control, the thing is, God is the one who is in control. He is just waiting for us to let Him move. He can't use hearts that withhold themselves from Him.

It is when we lay down our control, submitting our will, that we are able to be used in ways we never could have imagined. Take the scales of this Autonomous Christianity from your eyes and see the light of truth that is hidden within the covering of the Lord. Throw off the jejune faith that you have come to know. Become the vessel of anointing that God crafted you to be. Become the thing that the forces of hell tremble at when they see. Become the dwelling place of the Lord.

I understand that words on paper can sound great and inspiration can grip your heart in a holy fire, but what happens after a week goes by and you forget? How do you continue to live within the will of God; how do you continue to live with that fire burning in your soul beckoning you to fellowship with the Lord? The answer: stay in community.

All too often, we believe that we can go out on our own, in our own strength, and conquer the adversary. We start out walking with the Lord, and as we see His hand move in power in our own lives we can allow pride to creep in. We begin to claim credit for ourselves or lift up our flesh. We can take credit where it is due to the Lord.

We will eventually find ourselves overcome and overwhelmed, isolated as a product of our own strength. We will lean too much in our own ability, giving more credit to our flesh than is due. We will become prideful, believing that we do not need help or anyone else to partner with. We give way to our pride and isolate ourselves just as the enemy wants. We become useless and unable to advance the gospel because we are crippled by pride.

Or maybe we aren't prideful, maybe we are just fearful. We fear reaching out and so we confine ourselves to familiarity, never letting anyone see who we really are. We muzzle our mouths into submission with the fear that controls our mind. For some, we have been hurt in the past when we allowed ourselves to open up, for others, an intimate (not in the sense of love but as in close knit or deep) relationship with another person scares us because it requires commitment.

I'm sure there are other reasons for not wanting or fearing the community that is important in every believer's life. You see, we are made for community, for deep relationships with other believers. We see this modeled in the Garden of Eden when the Lord walked with Adam and had fellowship, we see it when Jesus taught His disciples, and we see it when Paul wrote letters to the church. Community is all throughout scripture.

I am sorry if you have been hurt in the past when you allowed yourself to have a deep relationship. I am sorry if your trust has been broken and betrayed. Community was not intended to harm you but we live in a broken world full of broken people that want you to hurt just as much as they do. There is good news though, Jesus came to repair what is broken.

We cannot live in the past and dwell on what has gone wrong because we will build up bitterness and anger. The enemy will have a field day with apathy and self-pity. What has happened will be used as a testimony for your future. You will be empowered, able to stand up and proclaim where you were, what happened, but what God has done in and through that circumstance.

Have you ever stepped on a bee or had a splinter? It hurts for a few days but eventually stops. I know this is shallow compared to being hurt in a relationship but stick with me. That bee sting or splinter will cause pain until the poison dissipates or the splinter is removed from your skin. This aspect is similar to a breach of trust.

When someone hurts you, be it physical or emotional, it hurts. You feel betrayed and wounded. It is extremely painful at first just like when a bee initially stings you or when that splinter first pierces your skin. After a few days or weeks the pain will subside but still be present. You know it is there because it throbs just like when your trust is broken and your guard is up, but then the bee sting will dissipate or the splinter will be removed.

In the same way, the Lord can take away the pain from that offense that has happened. The only difference is most people aren't going to think about that bee sting every time they go outside or flinch every time they see wood because of their splinter. So why do we dwell on what has happened, hindering ourselves from the blessings God has for us, instead of dwelling on what God is calling us to move into.

I understand that bee stings and splinters cannot come close to what we feel in emotions, but the principal of it is the same. Dwelling on past hurts will only create future hurts. It is exactly what the enemy wants, a crippled people overcome by fear and pains of the past. I don't know about you, but that makes me angry. It makes me want to call all of my friends and talk the night away just to laugh in the enemy's face.

Community can be considered one of the church's main keys. We thrive in community because we are surrounded by other believers, correcting and admonishing, encouraging and lifting up, fighting side by side for things of the kingdom. Without community, isolation sets in and creates a church that moves in each person's individual powers, which gives us a divided church.

You see, we are called to be set apart for the Lord's work, equipped to become leaders and messengers for the King, rooted in community, driven to see the hearts of men set free. We are created to display the image of a creator. We are to be separate from the rest, holy, no longer used for common things. We have been sanctified and consecrated to pursue the very heart of the Lord.

"But as He who called you is holy, you also be holy in all your conduct, because it is written, "Be holy for I am holy."

1 Peter 1:15-16

God is a holy God. At first glance, we associate this fact with joy, but the fact that God is holy should scare us. For if God is holy He must be righteous and we are by no means righteous. A holy God must have justice, and for the unjustified man that means death. A perfect God cannot associate Himself with evil and that is why Jesus was sent in the form of a man. Jesus is the door to a holy God.

To describe or even define holiness is an arduous task that I fear man will never be able to fully explain much less completely comprehend. Holiness is not simply an attribute of God, it is the thing that encompasses all of God's attributes. To be holy is to be set apart, separated, consecrated, completely given over to the things of the Lord.

So while we can never claim holiness within the boundaries of our own power, we can gain it through Christ. You see, in the same way that Jesus was consecrated, set apart and undone for kingdom things, we are called to do the same. If holiness is being consecrated before the Lord, forsaking everything we know for the advancement of the gospel, and a command from the Lord, why do we not walk in it?

I know and you know when someone is authentic with their beliefs. It is not hard to pick a faker out of a crowd. The question is, what are you? Are you authentic in your beliefs; do you passionately seek the face of the Lord, setting yourself apart in consecration each day? Or are you just a man who is content to bear a title but not Christ, just an imitator of the real thing?

People will know who or what you truly love because it will be evident in your actions. Is it evident that you are living in community? Have you set yourself apart, been consecrated, only fully giving yourself to the advancement of the kingdom? Is God your God or is He just a good luck charm that you rub when life knocks you down?

I will not remind you of sin just for the sake of it. I will remind you what the Scriptures say because submission to God's word is what makes the enemy tremble with fear and free your heart from the distractions of this world. We were bought with a price. Don't waste the sacrifice of your Savior. He seeks a generation of warriors that will stand for His name regardless of the world's persecution.

God will stamp His seal upon those who forsake their own lives for Him. He will empower them and they will be separate, set apart for His works. The enemy will tremble at their presence and fall before them because they have been anointed by their King. For God has claimed the hearts of those who love Him and by their obedience He will move mountains, part seas, crush the head of the enemy, and glorify His name.

So now it is clear what a Christian should look like, act like, and be known as. We are known by our harvest, created in the image of a holy God, called to be separate, and built for community. We should become undone when in the presence of our Lord, completely taken by His glory. To live in His presence is life, to move in His spirit is anointing, and to run to the nations is His commissioning. We were created to live in complete abandonment to the Lord. When we are able to do this, we catch a glimpse of what eternity on earth looks like.

So analyze your current walk with the Lord. Are you seeking His face daily, asking Him for His guidance? Are you hungry for His word, driven to see His kingdom advanced? Are you walking in community and building up the body of Christ? Are you setting yourself apart before the Lord asking that He have His way in your life? Are you completely surrendered to the Lord?

The Only Thing That Matters

So now what? We have analyzed what is happening in our culture and what Christians should look like, but what comes next? Well, the next step is finding courage. You see, we can love God with all of our heart, walk with Him every day, and live in community, but if we allow ourselves to become confined to our "Christian bubble" we will squander the opportunities given to us to share Christ with others.

We live in a hurting world that is constantly seeking the fulfillment of purpose, the promise of something that is worth living for. As the body, it is our job and joy to share that missing piece in their lives. We have found something worth living for, and we should be driven to see others find the same hope that we have. We were redeemed from brokenness, raised up in power, and are now sent to the broken to see the power of God move in their lives.

You see, we have to realize something that will completely offend our flesh and crush our pride: nothing except the will of God matters. Let me say that again. Nothing except the will of God matters. At the end of life, everything will fade away. Riches, social groups, position, love, passions, they will no longer matter. Earthly deeds and heroics will amount to nothing, riches will burn up as chaff, your friend circles will be of no importance, not even the love you have for another human being will amount to the level of devotion you will feel toward Christ.

You know what will matter, that conversation you had with your neighbor that ultimately got him to listen, then come to church, and later on accept Christ. At the end of life, when all is said and done, only two things will matter: your salvation and the salvation of those who saw Christ in you. The question is, did others see Christ in you?

Every day we walk through life, opportunities are presented, some accepted and some passed over, but at the end of the day you will sit down believing that you did a good job. At least, according to the advancement of the kingdom you will believe you did a good job. Contentment will come from those twenty seconds you prayed in public over your food, or that quick reference to the Bible that you quickly moved on from the very moment it left your lips, or maybe you are satisfied with that quick prayer you said as you slipped out the door before work.

We make a mistake in our lives. We use uncommon things for common purposes. We take what is holy, righteous, and good, and we squander it if we are not careful. It is as if we use a gold brick for nothing more than a paperweight. Are the advances you make for the kingdom sincere, or are they just habits and rituals that have fallen into a mundane routine?

What would your life be like without Jesus? What if prayer and the Bible were taken from you, stripped away and restricted? Where would you be if God had not stepped in and offered forgiveness? Or what if you knew there was a God but He offered no sanctification, no justification, no salvation, no hope for your future? What if you were left to your sin, unable to justify yourself before God? What would your life look like?

Do you see what I am saying now? In American culture we have turned God, His word, His promises, His being into a ritual. We have placed an uncommon, priceless object in a position only meant for common things. We do not see the significance of Jesus' sacrifice with eyes full of wonder and love so much so that we find ourselves pulled to our knees weeping with thanksgiving pouring from our tongues.

Instead, we see a twenty second prayer over our food as an obligation instead of a privilege. When will the scales fall from our eyes and expose this gray gospel for the crutch to men that it has become? We have twisted holiness all for the sake of saving face and sustaining comfort. Throw off the suppositions and guidelines of man's interpretations and read the Scriptures for yourself. Heed wisdom and direction, but know what the Bible says.

How are Christians supposed to witness and evangelize if we have no idea how to accurately interpret it? Better yet, how are we supposed to share Jesus with others when we don't even have a relationship with Him ourselves? We can't. We cannot be His hands and feet if we cannot recognize His hands and feet.

Equip yourself so that you can be used for the kingdom. You can be an educated Christian and still do less than an orphan in a third world country because the difference is that you are comfortable sitting back rendering yourself ineffective while that orphan is running after Heaven because he realizes that his King is the only thing that matters.

It seems as if most Christians today are not concerned with the hurting hearts of lost people as much as they should be. There is a shifted priority streak that has taken place, or maybe it is just selfishness. Our hearts long for Jesus but our tongue only professes wishes instead of plans. Our faith is nothing without the evidence of works.

In order to advance the gospel, there must be a people willing to lay down everything and run to the nations. There cannot be hesitancy or inconsistency, there can only be the kingdom. Jesus gave His all to save men that despised Him. The same men that killed Him were forgiven by the blood they shed. If Jesus could die for a filthy traitor such as ourselves, then why do we not offer up our lives to Him? He bought us with His blood and redeemed us from the inheritance of men, we owe Him everything.

In some aspects, I believe we are afraid. We are afraid to submit our all, extend our hands toward Heaven, and say, "Here I am, use me." We are afraid of men. We are afraid of what men will do to us when we proclaim the name of Jesus. We always think about persecution, torture or martyrdom, we never think about what the Father has planned.

We will see through the eyes of men, unable to see the future of events that God sees. We see crowds of angry people seeking our death when the Lord sees oceans of people praising His name. We hear angry shouts of hate when the Lord hears the cry of hearts that beat after His own. We limit our boundaries when God calls us forward and sends us to the unknown. The key in all of this is trust.

We are finite, meaning we are limited. God is not. He is omniscient or all-knowing. God can see what will happen before it happens. When He calls us out and sends us to do what might seem impossible or dangerous, it is because He can see the big picture which might require us in order to advance His kingdom. We can have assurance that God has us in His hand and that in His will we are safe even though the situation and circumstances might be dangerous.

So, we must have courage. We must be willing to take a stand for our beliefs even when we are the only one. It is a mandate to us to stand for what is true so that through our testimony men will see and believe. Our lives can match Scripture and we can walk according to the Word, but if we lack the resolve to see the kingdom advance, the strength to stand and fight for kingdom things, our beliefs are dead because there is no fruit.

So we need courage, but where does it come from? Courage comes from loving God above all else and maintaining the drive to see His kingdom advanced. We place God or should place God above everything else in our lives so obeying Him instead of bowing to men will not be a problem because we will see God as worthy of the most importance.

Courage can also come from the Scriptures. When accurately studied, interpreted, and applied, the Bible will strengthen our faith and build up our resolve. In order to stand in this day and age we must be rooted in something. Being rooted in God's Word will keep us in line with His will and give us a foundation to stand upon. We will have proof for our words and a surety in them.

While there are many ways to find courage, I will only name the biggest three and the third one is community. Boldness comes more easily when you are surrounded by friends. There is strength in numbers, not force, but numbers. We have more courage when we know that there are others by our side that stand for the same beliefs.

Community is used to build up, to edify the body. Without it, we are isolated and easily overcome. However, for community to take place there must be unity. There must be a willingness to step out of your comfort zone and into the messed up lives of others in order to have community. There must first be outreach then relationship. Community is not built overnight or in a few short weeks, it is the commitment to see others set free and grow in the Lord no matter how much time is required or how much you are inconvenienced.

You cannot have community without hard work because community is built upon relationships and relationships require time and inconvenience. We must view this with the perspective of the Lord in mind. We must see people as heirs or potential heirs to the kingdom. We cannot look on as if the person before us is filthy with sin while we are white as snow.

Are we not all sinners before the eyes of the Lord? Will we not stand before Him one day to attest to the wickedness of our hands? We are all in the same boat, and its sinking. The only difference, a man has seen us flailing in the water as we sink and is reaching out to pull us to safety. It is often hard to think about our own life and compare it to what we find repulsive and of lesser quality than our current state.

Thing is, in God's eyes, we are all sinners that have fallen short even though there is forgiveness to be found. Sin is not weighed by severity as in human understanding, but by the rejection and separation from the Lord. When we can finally see ourselves in this aspect, we will realize that there is not a single one of us who can claim righteousness by his own accord. We are all in need of a savior.

When we can place ourselves on the same level as the man that, in our eyes, is nothing more than a filthy sinner unworthy of our time, we are humbled. The good news is we can see ourselves in the filth that we were redeemed from and then look at what the Lord has done for us. The goal to using this perspective is that we no longer see a caste system or social cliques, we see God's creation and realize that nothing matters except the Gospel.

The point I am driving at is this: God loves you in the same way He loves that unsaved person in your life and He expects you to love them more than yourself. Throw off the petty cliques and catty attitudes that you learned from your high school years. Community is not a caste system or even a gated community when the Lord is concerned.

Community is as close as family. As the church, the body of Christ, we are called to live in community and view ourselves as of no better than our brothers. We have to see people with the Lord's eyes, not our own. How can we advance the kingdom when we cannot even view our brothers as of equal importance to ourselves?

So you have courage which involves loving God, knowing Scripture, and living in community, but where does courage lead? Well, courage leads you to people. You will be driven to evangelism because that is what the Lord requires of His people, the advancement of His Gospel. Everything we have talked about in the previous chapters will lead you right back to evangelism.

We are made to love Jesus with all that we are and we are made to carry His name to the nations regardless of the cost involved. God seeks hearts that are willing to do His will. If we can love God more than life itself we have found something more precious than any riches on this earth could buy. We have found purpose.

The key is abandoning our advancements and escaping the entanglement of a compromising Christianity. As a church, we need more abandonment. We need to abandon self, abandon cultural ties, abandon our will, and submit. The whole concept of abandoning what we deem familiar and comfortable is difficult because it goes against our flesh. Thing is, the kingdom will always contradict our flesh because what is holy cannot compromise with what is unholy.

We must realize that we are all called to be ambassadors to the nations, a people who are willing to walk through great danger to spread word of a loving God who sent His only son as a substitutionary sacrifice. Life itself is counted as a cost to the Gospel. We are mistaken if we believe that God will not call us to do dangerous things. God will call us to walk where no one else will because He cares for the hearts of people and while we might be in dangerous places we will be safe in God's will.

As a church it is our job to evangelize. We are called and led to fight for the hearts of people, to fight for advances of the kingdom. We are called to testify to the Lord's goodness. There is no way to tip toe around this last component. I guess I am trying to articulate this last and final point correctly before I wrap this book up. Thing is, when the day is over and all is said and done, there is only one thing that is eternal, life changing, and faithful. That thing, rather that man, is Jesus Christ.

From the moment we first take in a breath to the moment where we let out our last, we are given chances to glorify our God. Without Him there would be no earth, no human race, no reason for life. God is the creator and perfecter of life. He is Almighty God, besides Him none can compare. Yet, in all of His might and glory, He created man.

Intricately created to bear the image of the Creator, man was formed as the breath of the Lord filed his lungs. When man fell short of perfection and separated himself from his Creator he was left to pay for his actions. Creation betrayed its Creator but the Creator remained faithful still. Our just and loving God owed us nothing except justice. We were to be separated from the Lord for eternity because of our trespass, but God still remained faithful.

God sent Jesus to earth. The son of God, perfection's source, came to live our life, be tempted as we are, and ultimately take our place on the cross. God gave up His only son to atone for the sins of our hands knowing that we will never reach perfection and we will continue to sin because of our nature. Jesus submitted to the Father's will and stood in our place of judgment.

And so the Creator willingly listened to the cries of His son while nails were driven into flesh and out the back of a wooden cross. The Creator turned His face as His son bled out. The Creator gave up His own for a creation that had rejected Him. The greatest gift that mankind has ever been given came from the greatest sacrifice that mankind will ever know.

Through the death of Jesus, a road was paved. A gap was bridged from us to God by Jesus. We were given the choice to choose God, to choose repentance and salvation. This is the story, the history, that we have inherited. Our commission is so simple, take what we have been given and multiply until our Creator calls us home.

We are human, finite at best. Eternity awaits and there are only two places to spend it. At the end of life, we will look back and see the years pass by in memories. We will see moments fly by whether they are fleeting or eternal, and we will see the fruit of our lives. The only thing to leave this earth will be the regenerate souls that chose to call upon the name of their Creator. Nothing else will matter except those souls.

So from life's first breath to deaths last exhale, Jesus is all that matters. We were purchased from a debt that only one could pay and our life was bought with blood. We are not our own. This is a foreign concept for most but it is true. Jesus paid our price with the very life that sustained Him. He gave His all knowing that some would still despise Him.

He gave life back to us so who are we to withhold ourselves from Him. Our lives are counted as cost to the kingdom. We are not our own. I am not my own and you are not your own. We are ambassadors for our Lord, the creation of a Creator, and the servants of a King. We are privileged with tools to equip us such as the Bible, authentic community, and the Holy Spirit.

Our life should revolve around the Lord. Everything else will fall into alignment when Jesus is our priority. Life is not about graduating from the most prestigious school, landing a great job, starting a family, climbing society's ladder, or retiring in the Bahamas. Life is about Jesus. Life is about running to the call of the Creator and carrying His message to the ends of the earth.

Acknowledgments

I am extremely grateful for all the help I have received in writing this book. I wish to thank everyone who contributed whether they know if they did or not. I would like to start out by thanking my family: Jim and Rachel Shelton, James Shelton, Laura Klostermeier, Ray and Kathryn Laffoon, Jared klostermeier, Donny and Angela Klostermeier, Sophia Klostermeier, Juliana Klostermeier, and Brenda Dollarhide. This book would never have been finished without your support and encouragement.

I would like to thank Chadrick Owens, my sophomore language teacher, for willingly taking on the arduous task of proofreading my drafts. P.S. (I made sure I got all the mistakes out and my grammar has improved…..I think.)

I would like to thank Ron Gleaves for inspiring me to not do what's expected but what's inspected and for starting the whole idea of this book even though he had no idea. I send a big thanks out to my uncle, Jim Laffoon, as well. You also had a big deal to do with the start of this book.

Thanks to all of my church friends and leaders and please don't get offended if I don't name you all because there are way too many names...but thank you New Song Christian Fellowship and Graceland.

Thanks to all of my teachers and friends at Zion Christian Academy.

A big shout out to my Doctrine buddies, Sean Richardson, Joseph O'Brian, and Daniel Nichols who never hesitated to ask the unanswerable questions. Thank you for sharpening iron with me and never failing to ask questions which exceeded the finite mind.

www.ingramcontent.com/pod-product-compliance
Ingram Content Group UK Ltd.
Pitfield, Milton Keynes, MK11 3LW, UK
UKHW020221250726
13967UKWH00001B/124

9 781329 388796